Cheers for the Cheetahs

by Kim Whiting

illustrated by
Aleksey Ivanov

PEARSON

Scott
Foresman

Editorial Offices: Glenview, Illinois • Parsippany, New Jersey • New York, New York
Sales Offices: Needham, Massachusetts • Duluth, Georgia • Glenview, Illinois
Coppell, Texas • Ontario, California • Mesa, Arizona

Every effort has been made to secure permission and provide appropriate credit for photographic material. The publisher deeply regrets any omission and pledges to correct errors called to its attention in subsequent editions.

Unless otherwise acknowledged, all photographs are the property of Scott Foresman, a division of Pearson Education.

Illustrations by Aleksey Ivanov

Photograph 16 Associated Press

ISBN: 0-328-13427-9

10 V0FL 15 14 13 12 11

Hannah Adams held her breath. The ball bounced hard on the edge of the basketball hoop and rolled around the rim.

"Please," whispered Hannah. "Go in." The ball wobbled, tipped, and fell off the hoop. Hannah sighed. She had missed again.

"Try it this way," said Ellie. She bounced the ball once, shot, and sank it in the net.

"You make it look so easy," said Hannah. "It's not."

"Don't worry about it," said Ellie. "We have enough players to prove to Mr. Giddings how good we are. What we really need now is someone who can write. No one is better at that than you."

Hannah smiled at her friend. Ellie always knew what to say to make Hannah feel better. They were almost like sisters, except that they were so different.

Hannah was tall and not very graceful when she ran. Her feet always seemed to be in her way. Even so, Hannah loved sports. She never gave up trying to get better at them.

Ellie, on the other hand, was good at every sport she tried. She moved very quickly, just like a basketball player who would win an Olympic gold medal. In fact, that was her nickname: Goldie.

The two girls had been practicing their shots. They wanted to prove that the girls in their fourth-grade class could play basketball as well as any of the boys.

Mr. Giddings, their gym teacher, did not seem to think that was possible. He was the coach for the boys' basketball team. He never asked girls to join his winning team. He hardly ever noticed the girls. He always gave the boys more playing time than the girls during gym class.

"It's unbelievable," said Goldie one day after gym. She, Hannah, and some of the other girls were eating lunch together. "He doesn't even see us. We could skip gym and he'd never notice."

"How could he not notice you, Goldie?" marveled Hannah. "You're better than any of the boys. And Lizzie and Charlene are easily as good as Hakim and Freddy. We've got to show him. Maybe Ms. Clemens can help us." Ms. Clemens was the principal at Emberly Elementary.

As the girls talked, they began to make a plan.
"Hannah, you should write the letter to Ms.
Clemens," said Goldie finally. "You can explain
everything to her. She'll help us. Now, let's shoot
hoops until we can do it with our eyes shut."

That was how they had left it a few days
earlier. Now, Hannah's job was to convince Ms.
Clemens the girls needed help. She had spent all
afternoon thinking about what to say. Finally,
Hannah wrote the important letter.

Dear Ms. Clemens,

We need your help. In gym,
Mr. Giddings pays more attention to
the boys. The girls just sit around.
We want Mr. Giddings to give us a chance.
Can you please talk to him about this
problem? To prove how good we are, we
want to challenge the boys to a basketball
game. Would you be the referee? Thank you
very much.

Sincerely,
Hannah Adams and
the 4th-Grade Girls

The next day at school, Hannah delivered her letter. She spent the morning waiting nervously for an answer. Would Ms. Clemens be mad? Should Hannah have said those things about Mr. Giddings and gym class? Goldie told her not to worry. Ms. Clemens would understand. Suddenly, Hannah heard her name called over the intercom.

"Hannah Adams, please report to the office." Hannah gulped. Goldie flashed her a big smile.

"Go for it!" whispered Goldie. Hannah dragged herself out of her chair and slowly walked down to the office.

"Thank you for bringing this to my attention," said Ms. Clemens after Hannah sat down in her office. "I asked Mr. Giddings about it. He was speechless."

Of course he was, thought Hannah. *He doesn't even know he leaves the girls out.* She looked at the principal, expecting to be scolded.

"Mr. Giddings has agreed to let you organize a game, boys against girls," said Ms. Clemens with a big smile. "And I would be glad to be the ref."

"Wow!" Hannah exclaimed with surprise. "Thanks, Ms. Clemens."

The girls quickly burst into action. They first decided on a team name. They called themselves the Cheetahs, after the cats known for bursts of speed. They next made team jerseys dotted with cheetah spots.

Game day arrived. The whistle blew and the ball began to fly around the court. The Cheetahs had it. The boys got it. The Cheetahs stole it back.

The girls were leading, 23-22, when Hakim jumped for a shot. Hannah swatted the ball away and fouled him. The foul earned Hakim two free shots. Goldie looked at Hannah in alarm. There were just thirty seconds left. They had worked too hard to lose the game now.

Swish! Hakim sank the first shot perfectly in the net, tying the score. But on the second shot, the ball bounced off the backboard and onto the rim. Freddy dashed in to grab the rebound. Just then, Goldie appeared out of nowhere. She was gone in a flash, taking the ball with her. She darted up the court. With one second left she stopped, aimed, and shot. The ball hit the rim, tottered, and tumbled into the net as the whistle blew. The Cheetahs had won!

Mr. Giddings bounded down the bleachers and onto the middle of the court. He was wondering how he had missed such talent when it was right under his nose.

"That was fantastic!" he said, shaking Goldie's hand. "I'm starting a co-ed team at the Y. Will the Cheetahs join me?"

Goldie winked at Hannah.

"If you let us practice during gym," she said.

"You bet," said Mr. Giddings.

Title IX

Before 1972 girls had far fewer chances to play sports than boys did. That year, the federal government passed a law known as Title IX. This law bans gender discrimination in colleges that get money from the U.S. government. One result of the new law was that colleges began to offer girls many more athletic choices.

As a result, interest in girl's basketball soared. In 1972 fewer than 135,000 girls played the game in high school. By 1994 that number had more than tripled. Two years later, in 1996, the American women's basketball team won a gold medal at the Olympics.

The New York Liberty and the Los Angeles Sparks are professional women's basketball teams.